Bread Machine Cooking

The Ultimate Guide to Bread Machine
Bread Baking

Over 24 Bread Machine Recipes You Will Love!

By

Martha Stephenson

License Notes

No part of this Book can be reproduced in any form or by any means including print, electronic, scanning or photocopying unless prior permission is granted by the author.

All ideas, suggestions and guidelines mentioned here are written for informative purposes. While the author has taken every possible step to ensure accuracy, all readers are advised to follow information at their own risk. The author cannot be held responsible for personal and/or commercial damages in case of misinterpreting and misunderstanding any part of this Book

Table of Contents

Introduction

Who doesn't love the taste of freshly made bread nowadays? There's just something about a freshly made a loaf of bread or hot dinner rolls to serve with your dinner meal to make it complete. From Focaccia to sourdough bread there are a variety of different bread recipes that you can make. However, there are some people out there who do not want to make bread by hand as it takes too much time. If you are this type of person than the best thing to do is utilize a bread machine.

A bread machine makes making bread a simple and fun task to do. Not only do you not have to worry about exhausting yourself in order to make bread, but you can literally make it within a couple of minutes.

If you are a huge fan of bread machines and breads in general, then this is a perfect book for you. Inside of this book you will discover over 25 is the most delicious bread machine recipes that you will ever find today. You will also find a few helpful tips to making your bread recipes within your bread machine so that you can make the most out of your nifty kitchen tool.

So, what are you waiting for?

Let's get baking!

Benefits to Owning Your Own Bread Machine

If you love to make freshly made bread and already own a bread machine than this is a perfect section for you to read. In the sectional learn about the various benefits to using a bread machine over making your bread by hand so that you can see exactly how nifty this little tool can be.

1. Can Come in Handy When You Need It

This is a great and nifty little tool to use when you need an extra oven on hand especially during the holiday season. We have all been there. Having to juggle multiple dishes to make one huge fantastic meal during the holidays. This is when your bread machine can come in handy as you can use it to make rolls, turkey, cranberries, or even stuffing.

2. Does Not Add Extra Heat to Your Kitchen

When using a bread machine, you never have to worry about adding any extra heat to your kitchen. This is especially important during the summer months when it can become sweltering hot in a small amount of time. A bread machine is usually completely self-enclosed and always stays cool to the touch even when you are baking bread in it. So you never have to worry about overheating your kitchen during the hot summer months.

3. Save Yourself on Electricity

Whether you are baking something small such as a small pumpkin bread or making something as large as a huge focaccia you can always use your bread machine without having to worry about raising your electric bill in the process. A bread machine can help you conserve energy instead of using your oven and can help save you money in your bank account in the long run.

4. Can Help Finish Cooking Dishes by Itself

If you use the jam cycle on your bread machine it is great to finish putting up things such as various dips or even dessert dishes. What this means is that you can set your dish right into your bread machine and walk off until it is done.

5. Incredibly Easy to Clean Up

When it comes to using your bread machine you never really have to worry about clean up as it is almost non-existent in this machine. All that you really have to do is scrub your bread machine container with an adequate amount of soapy hot water and rinse it and you are set to go.

A Few Helpful Bread Machine Cooking Tips

If you are new to using your bread machine and still do not have enough experience to make your own delicious bread recipes on your own, then this is the section you will love. Inside of the section you will find a couple of useful tips to making of the most delicious bread recipes you can within your bread machine.

1. Be Mindful of How You Use Your Ingredients

The first thing you want to do is make sure that you are always mindful of the order that you put your ingredients into your bread machine. Most machines require you to start with your liquids before moving onto your dry ingredients. The very last ingredient you'll want to add into your bread machine is yeast and to do this you want to make sure you make a small indentation into your dough for this to go in to.

Not only will this help to ensure that none of your ingredients are mixed before they are required to but it will ensure that you make each and every bread loaf as delicious as possible with this machine.

2. Be Aware of the Type of Flour That You Use

Most inexperienced bread makers are under the impression that all flours are created equal. This is not the case with bread. For the best and tastiest results, you need to make sure that you use only bread flour instead of all-purpose flour. Bread flour has a much higher protein level and contains gluten that is necessary for your bread to achieve its crispiness. Using all-purpose flour will not achieve the desired baking results.

3. If You Are Not Successful in Making Bread, Your Flour May Not Be Fresh

For the most successful bread recipes you'll need to ensure that your flour is as fresh as possible. Most of the time you may begin to achieve several different failures when it comes to baking your bread in your bread machine such as your bread collapsing during the baking process or your bread not coming out as crispy as you would have hoped. This is often due to the fact that the flour you are using is not fresh or is not being stored properly.

If this is the case, you will need to use more flour and this time you will need to make sure that it is stored properly and it is as fresh as possible.

4. If You Are Watching Your Fat Intake...

If you are the type of person that is currently on a diet or wants to watch the amount of fat that they are taking in on a daily basis, then you will want to make sure that you substitute your butter or oil for something else. I highly recommend substituting it for apple sauce or butter powder as it help to give bread a superior taste once made in the bread machine.

5. Don't Worry About the Different Cycles

Most inexperienced bread machine bakers will often panic at seeing all of the different cycles that comes with their bread machine. You may have settings varying between French, whole wheat or sweet variety. Don't worry about all of these settings as most of the time you will be only using a basic setting and your bread will come out tasting just fine.

Delicious Bread Machine Recipes

Easy Ciabatta Bread

While there are a few bread machine recipes out there that are hard to make, this is not one of those recipes. With the help of your bread machine, making this bread is easier than ever and I know you will love the taste of it.

Makes: 24 Servings

Total Prep Time: 1 Hour and 55 Minutes

Ingredients:

- 1 ½ Cups of Water, Warm
- 1 ½ tsp. of Salt, For Taste
- 1 tsp. of Sugar, White
- 1 Tbsp. of Olive Oil, Extra Virgin Variety
- 3 ¼ Cups of Flour, Bread Variety
- 1 ½ tsp. of Yeast, Active Variety

Directions:

1. The first thing that you will want to do is add all of your ingredients into your bread maker according to the directions suggested by the manufacturer.

2. Once your dough is completely mixed together and sticky to the touch, place onto a generously floured surface and cover with some plastic wrap. Allow to sit out for at least 15 minutes.

3. Meanwhile lightly flour two separate large sized baking sheets.

4. Then separate your dough into 2 even sized pieces and form into an oval shape. Place onto your baking sheets and dust with some flour. Cover with some plastic wrap and allow to rise for the next 45 minutes.

5. Next preheat your oven to 425 degrees.

6. After this time mist your loaves with some water and place into your oven to bake until golden brown in color. This should take at least 25 to 30 minutes.

7. After this time remove from heat and allow to cool before serving.

Steakhouse Style Wheat Bread

Originally this was a recipe honed from a popular copycat steakhouse chain recipe but now you are able to make this delicious and popular bread within the comfort of your own home.

Makes: 8 Servings

Total Prep Time: 3 Hours and 10 Minutes

Ingredients:

- ¾ Cup of Water, Warm
- 1 Tbsp. of Butter, Soft
- ¼ Cup of Honey, Raw
- ½ tsp. of Salt, For Taste
- 1 tsp. of Coffee, Instant Variety
- 1 Tbsp. of Cocoa Powder, Unsweetened Variety
- 1 Tbsp. of Sugar, White
- 1 Cup of Flour, Bread Variety
- 1 Cup of Flour, Whole Wheat Variety
- 1 ½ tsp. of Yeast, Active Variety

Directions:

1. The first thing that you will want to do is add all of your ingredients into your bread maker according to the directions suggested by the manufacturer.

2. Once your dough is completely mixed together and sticky to the touch, place onto a generously floured surface and cover with some plastic wrap. Allow to sit out for at least one hour.

3. Next preheat your oven to 425 degrees.

4. Place your loaf into your oven to bake until golden brown in color. This should take at least 40 to 60 minutes.

5. After this time remove from heat and allow to cool before serving.

Bread Machine Style Challah

If you are looking for an easy bread machine recipe to make, this is a great one to try out for yourself. For the best results I highly recommend only using the light setting on your bread machine.

Makes: 12 Servings

Total Prep Time: 3 Hours and 5 Minutes

Ingredients:

- ¾ Cup of Milk, Warm
- 2 Eggs, Large in Size and Beaten Thoroughly
- 3 Tbsp. of Butter, Soft
- 3 Cups of Flour, Bread Variety
- ¼ Cup of Sugar, White
- 1 ½ tsp. of Salt, For Taste
- 1 ½ tsp. of Yeast, Active Variety

Directions:

1. The first thing that you will want to do is add all of your ingredients into your bread maker according to the directions suggested by the manufacturer.

2. Once your dough is completely mixed together and sticky to the touch, place onto a generously floured surface and cover with some plastic wrap. Allow to sit out for at least 15 minutes.

3. Then bake according to your preference.

Tasty Banana Nut Bread

If you are a huge fan of banana nut bread, then this is certainly one bread machine recipe that you need to try making for yourself. It is absolutely delicious and will melt in your mouth with every bite.

Makes: 10 Servings

Total Prep Time: 2 Hours

Ingredients:

- ½ Cup of Butter, Soft
- 2/3 Cup of Milk, Whole and Warm
- 2 Eggs, Large in Size and Beaten Thoroughly
- 2 ½ Cups of Flour, All Purpose Variety
- 1 Cup of Sugar, White
- 2 ½ tsp. of Baker's Style Baking Powder
- ½ tsp. of Baker's Style Baking Soda
- 1 tsp. of Salt, For Taste
- 2/3 Cup of Bananas, Fresh and Fully Mashed
- ½ Cup of Walnuts, Finely Chopped

Directions:

1. The first thing that you will want to do is grease your bread machine with some cooking spray.

2. Then add all of your ingredients into your bread maker according to the directions suggested by the manufacturer.

3. Once your dough is completely mixed together and sticky to the touch, place onto a generously floured surface and cover with some plastic wrap. Allow to sit out for at least 20 minutes.

4. Place your loaf into a baking pan and bake in your oven for the next hour to hour and a half or until completely baked through.

Classic Hot Cross Buns

This dish makes for a sweet tasty and absolutely mouthwatering bread recipe that you won't be able to resist. This is a great and tasty treat to make when you want to impress a group of your friends or family.

Makes: 12 Servings

Total Prep Time: 3 Hours and 30 Minutes

Ingredients:

- ¾ Cup of Water, Warm
- 3 Tbsp. of Butter, Soft
- 1 Tbsp. of Milk, Instant and Powdered Variety
- ¼ Cup of Sugar, White
- 3/8 tsp. of Salt, For Taste
- 1 Egg, Large in Size and Beaten
- 1 Egg, White Only
- 3 Cups of Flour, All Purpose Variety
- 1 Tbsp. of Yeast, Active and Dry Variety
- ¾ Cup of Currants, Dried Variety
- 1 tsp. of Cinnamon, Ground
- 1 Egg, Yolk Only
- 2 Tbsp. of Water, Warm
- ½ Cup of Sugar, Confectioner's Variety
- ¼ tsp. of Vanilla, Pure
- 2 tsp. of Mil, Whole and Warm

Directions:

1. Place your first 10 ingredients into your bread machine and press the start button.

2. During the last 5 minutes of the bread machine process, add in your next 2 ingredients. Then leave your dough in your machine to rise for the next 5 minutes

3. Transfer your dough onto a lightly floured surface and allow to rest for the next 10 minutes.

4. After this time shape your dough into 12 even sized balls and then place into a large sized generously greased baking dish. Cover with some plastic wrap and allow to rise for the next 35 to 40 minutes.

5. Next mix together your yolk and water together until thoroughly mixed together. Bush this mixture on your dough balls.

6. Place into your oven to bake at 375 degrees for the next 20 minutes. After this time remove from your oven and place on a wire rack until completely cooled.

7. While your balls are cooling make your glaze. To do this mix your last 3 ingredients together and brush onto your cooled buns in an X shape. Serve whenever you are ready.

Simple White Bread

If you are a huge fan of white bread, then this is the perfect bread machine recipe for you. For the most delicious results serve this bread with some butter or warm jam during your next dinner meal.

Makes: 12 Servings

Total Prep Time: 3 Hours and 5 Minutes

Ingredients:

- 1 ¼ Cups of Milk, Warm
- 3 Cups of Flour, All Purpose Variety
- 1 ½ Tbsp. of Sugar, White
- 1 ½ tsp. of Salt, For Taste
- 2 Tbsp. of Butter, Soft
- 2 tsp. of Yeast, Active and Dry

Directions:

1. The first thing that you will want to do is grease your bread machine with some cooking spray.

2. Then add all of your ingredients into your bread maker according to the directions suggested by the manufacturer.

3. Once your dough is completely mixed together and sticky to the touch, place onto a generously floured surface and cover with some plastic wrap. Allow to sit out for at least 20 minutes.

4. Place your loaf into a baking pan and bake in your oven for the next hour to hour and a half or until completely baked through.

5. Remove from oven and allow to cool before serving and slicing. Enjoy.

Bread Machine Style Bagels

If you are a huge fan of bagels, then this is one recipe that you need to try for yourself. These bagels are relatively easy to make and for the tastiest results feel free to use whatever toppings you wish.

Makes: 9 Servings

Total Prep Time: 3 Hours and 55 Minutes

Ingredients:

- 1 Cup of Water, Warm
- 1 ½ tsp. of Salt, For Taste
- 2 Tbsp. of Sugar, White
- 3 Cups of Flour, Bread Variety
- 2 ¼ tsp. of Yeast, Dry and Active
- 3 Quarts of Water, Boiling
- 3 Tbsp. of Sugar, White
- 1 Tbsp. of Cornmeal
- 1 Egg, White Part Only
- 3 Tbsp. of Poppy Seeds, Optional

Directions:

1. Place your first 5 ingredients into your bread machine according to the directions listed in your user's manual.

2. Once your bread cycle is complete, place your dough onto a lightly floured surface.

3. Next bring at least 3 quarts of water to a boil and then add in your sugar.

4. Cut your dough into 9 equal sized pieces and roll each piece into a small sized ball. Flatten each of these balls and poke a hole right into the center and enlarge the circle using your thumb.

5. Cover each of your newly formed bagels with a clean piece of moist cloth and allow to rest for the next 10 minutes.

6. After this time sprinkle your cornmeal over an ungreased baking sheet.

7. Carefully transfer your bagels to your boiling water and allow to boil for at least 1 minute. After this time drain your bagels on a clean paper towel and transfer to your baking sheet.

8. Top each bagel with a glaze of your egg whites and top with your favorite toppings.

9. Place into your oven to bake at 375 degrees for the next 20 to 25 minutes or until golden brown in color. Remove and allow to cool before serving.

Sweet Tasting Dinner Rolls

If you wish to serve the most delicious dinner rolls during your next family dinner, then this is the best recipe for you. These rolls are not only light, but they are sweet to taste, making it one dinner roll recipe you are going to want to make over and over again.

Makes: 16 Servings

Total Prep Time: 2 Hours and 20 Minutes

Ingredients:

- ½ Cup of Water, Warm
- ½ Cup of Milk, Warm
- 1 Egg, Large in Size and Beaten
- 1/3 Cup of Butter, Soft
- 1/3 Cup of Sugar, White
- 1 tsp. of Salt, For Taste
- 3 ¾ Cups of Flour, All Purpose Variety
- 1 Pack of Yeast, Active and Dry
- ¼ Cup of Butter, Soft

Directions:

1. The first thing that you will want to do is place your first 8 ingredients into your bread maker according to the directions suggested by the manufacturer.

2. Once your dough is completely mixed together and sticky to the touch, place onto a generously floured surface and divide your dough in half.

3. Next roll out each half of your dough until thick and spread at least ¼ cup of your butter over the top of each roll.

4. Cut each round into 8 equal sized rolls and roll into tight balls.

5. Cover your rolls with a clean kitchen towel and allow to rise in a warm place for the next hour.

6. While your rolls are rising, preheat your oven to 400 degrees.

7. After 1 hour place your rolls into your oven to bake for the next 10 to 15 minutes or until golden brown in color. Remove from oven and allow to cool slightly before serving.

Classic Bread Machine Pizza Dough

If you are making homemade pizza during your next dinner meal, then this is the best pizza dough recipe for you to make. Not only is it incredibly easy to make, but it will give your pizza that delicious taste that you won't be able to resist.

Makes: 6 Servings

Total Prep Time: 2 Hours and 34 Minutes

Ingredients:

- 1 Cup of Beer, Your Favorite Kind and Flat
- 2 Tbsp. of Butter, Soft
- 2 Tbsp. of Sugar, White
- 1 tsp. of Salt, For Taste
- 2 ½ Cups of Flour, All Purpose Variety
- 2 ¼ tsp. of Yeast, Dry and Active Variety

Directions:

1. The first thing that you will want to do is grease your bread machine with some cooking spray.

2. Then add in all of your ingredients into your bread maker according to the directions suggested by the manufacturer.

3. Once your dough is completely mixed together and sticky to the touch, place onto a generously floured surface and brush with some olive oil. Allow to stand for at least 15 minutes.

4. While your dough is resting preheat your oven to 400 degrees.

5. Next spread your desired sauce over your dough and top with your desired toppings.

6. Place into your oven to bake until lightly brown in color and crispy. This should take at least 25 minutes at most.

7. Remove from oven and allow to cool before serving.

Traditional French Baguettes

This is a classic bread recipe that I know you are going to love making. This is a great type of bread to use to make classic subs or to serve along a piping hot bowl of soup.

Makes: 12 Servings

Total Prep Time: 1 Hour and 50 Minutes

Ingredients:

- 1 Cup of Water, Warm
- 2 ½ Cups of Flour, Bread Variety
- 1 Tbsp. of Sugar, White
- 1 tsp. of Salt, For Taste
- 1 ½ tsp. of Yeast, Active and Dry Variety
- 1 Egg, Yolk Only
- 1 Tbsp. of Water

Directions:

1. The first thing that you will want to do is grease your bread machine with some cooking spray.

2. Then add in your first 5 ingredients into your bread maker according to the directions suggested by the manufacturer.

3. Once your dough is completely mixed together and sticky to the touch, cover your bowl with some plastic wrap and allow to rise for the next 30 minutes or until it has fully doubled in size.

4. Next punch down your dough and place onto a lightly floured surface. Roll into a large sized rectangle and then cut in half.

5. Roll your both doughs tightly and roll back and forth to taper the ends. Make diagonal slashes into your loaves and allow to rest for the next 30 to 40 minutes.

6. While your dough is resting preheat your oven to 375 degrees.

7. Then mix your egg yolk and remaining water together. Brush over the top of your loaves.

8. After your dough has risen place into your oven to bake for the next 20 to 25 minutes or until golden brown in color.

9. Remove from oven and allow to cool slightly before using.

Sweet Cinnamon Rolls

This is one of my personal favorite bread machine recipes and once you get a taste of them yourself, I know it will become your favorite too. The best part about them is the dough can be easily made in the comfort of your own home, making this one of the easiest cinnamon roll recipes that you will ever find.

Makes: 16 Servings

Total Prep Time: 2 Hours and 20 Minutes

Ingredients:

- ¼ Cup of Water, Room Temperature
- ¼ Cup of Butter, Melted
- ½ Pack of Vanilla Pudding Mix, Instant Variety
- 1 Cup of Milk, Warm
- 1 Egg, Room Temperature
- 1 Tbsp. of Sugar, White
- ½ tsp. of Salt, For Taste
- 4 Cups of Flour, Bread Variety
- 1 Pack of Yeast, Active and Dry
- ½ Cup of Butter, Soft
- 1 Cup of Brown Sugar, Light and Packed
- 4 tsp. of Cinnamon, Ground
- ¾ Cup of Pecans, Finely Chopped
- 1 Pack of Cream Cheese, Soft
- ¼ Cup of Butter, Soft

- 1 Cup of Sugar, Confectioners Variety
- ½ tsp. of Vanilla, Pure
- 1 ½ tsp. of Milk, Whole

Directions:

1. The first thing that you will want to do is grease your bread machine with some cooking spray.

2. Then add in first 9 ingredients into your bread maker according to the directions suggested by the manufacturer.

3. Once your dough is completely mixed together and sticky to the touch, place onto a generously floured surface and roll into a large sized rectangle. Spread your butter over the top of the dough.

4. Then use a small sized bowl and stir together your next 3 ingredients until evenly mixed.

5. Next sprinkle your light and packed brown sugar generously over your dough and butter a large sized baking dish with some butter.

6. Next roll up your dough into a log and slice into 16 equal sized pieces. Place into your pan and allow to rise for the next 45 minutes or until the rolls double in size.

7. While your dough is rising preheat your oven to 350 degrees.

8. After your rolls have risen place your rolls into your oven and bake until brown in color. This should take at least 15 to 20 minutes.

9. While your rolls are baking stir together your last 5 ingredients in a small sized bowl until evenly mixed and smooth in consistency.

10. After your rolls have become brown in color remove from oven and allow to cool completely. Then spread your premade frosting over your rolls and serve whenever you are ready.

Light Oat Bread

This is the perfect bread machine recipe if you are looking for something a little lighter and on the healthy side.

Makes: 12 Servings

Total Prep Time: 3 Hours and 5 Minutes

Ingredients:

- 1 ¼ Cups of Water, Warm
- 2 Tbsp. of Butter, Soft
- 1 tsp. of Salt, For Taste
- 3 Cups of Flour, All Purpose Variety
- ½ Cup of Oats, Rolled Variety
- 2 Tbsp. of Brown Sugar, Light and Packed
- 1 ½ tsp. of Yeast, Active and Dry

Directions:

1. The first thing that you will want to do is grease your bread machine with some cooking spray.

2. Then add all of your ingredients into your bread maker according to the directions suggested by the manufacturer.

3. Once your dough is completely mixed together and sticky to the touch, place onto a generously floured surface and cover with some plastic wrap. Allow to sit out for at least 20 to 35 minutes.

4. Place your loaf into a baking pan and bake in your oven for the next hour to hour and a half or until completely baked through.

Amish Style Bread

This is a delicious bread recipe that was originally adapted from a classic Amish recipe that I recently came across. It is so easy to make thanks to your own bread machine and tastes absolutely delicious.

Makes: 12 Servings

Total Prep Time: 4 Hours and 10 Minutes

Ingredients:

- 2 ¾ Cup of Flour, All Purpose Variety
- ¼ Cup of Oil, Canola Variety
- 1 tsp. of Yeast, Active and Dry Variety
- ¼ Cup of Sugar, White
- ½ tsp. of Salt, For Taste
- 18 Tbsp. of Water, Warm Variety

Directions:

1. The first thing that you will want to do is grease your bread machine with some cooking spray.

2. Then add all of your ingredients into your bread maker according to the directions suggested by the manufacturer.

3. Once your dough is completely mixed together and sticky to the touch, place onto a generously floured surface and cover with some plastic wrap. Allow to sit out for at least hour to hour and a half.

4. Place your loaf into a baking pan and bake in your oven for the next hour to hour and a half or until completely baked through.

Delicious Honey Wheat Sandwich Rolls

Just as the name implies this is a hearty and delicious country style sandwich roll recipe that you are going to want to use for every sandwich recipe you make. Feel free to freeze any extra that you may have to use for many days to come.

Makes: 14 Servings

Total Prep Time: 2 Hours and 45 Minutes

Ingredients:

- 1 ¼ Cups of Milk, Warm
- 1 Egg, Large in Size and Beaten
- 2 Tbsp. of Butter, Soft
- ¼ Cup of Honey, Raw
- ¾ tsp. of Salt, For Taste
- 2 ¾ Cup of Flour, Bread Variety
- 1 Cup of Flour, Whole Wheat Variety
- 1 ¼ tsp. of Yeast, Active and Dry Variety
- 2 Tbsp. of Butter, Fully Melted

Directions:

1. The first thing that you are going to want to do is place all of your ingredients into your bread maker according to the directions suggested by the manufacturer.

2. Once your dough is completely mixed together and sticky to the touch, place onto a generously floured surface and roll out until at least ¾ of an inch thick.

3. Then use a biscuit cutter and cut out at least 14 equal sized rolls.

4. Place onto an ungreased cookie sheet and cover with some plastic wrap. Allow to rise for the next hour.

5. While your biscuits are rising, preheat your oven to 350 degrees.

6. Once your rolls have finished rising place your rolls into your oven to bake for the next 10 to 15 minutes.

7. Once fully baked through remove from oven and allow to cool completely before using.

Portuguese Style Sweet Bread

Here is yet another sweet tasting bread recipe that I know you are going to fall in love with. It is so sweet to taste; this bread will help to satisfy the strongest sweet tooth.

Makes: 12 Servings

Total Prep Time: 3 Hours and 5 Minutes

Ingredients:

- 1 Cup of Milk, Whole
- 1 Egg, Large in Size and Beaten
- 2 Tbsp. of Butter, Soft
- 1/3 Cup of Sugar, White
- ¾ tsp. of Salt, For Taste
- 3 Cups of Flour, Bread Variety
- 2 ½ tsp. of Yeast, Active and Dry Variety

Directions:

1. The first thing that you will want to do is grease your bread machine with some cooking spray.

2. Then add all of your ingredients into your bread maker according to the directions suggested by the manufacturer.

3. Once your dough is completely mixed together and sticky to the touch, place onto a generously floured surface and cover with some plastic wrap. Allow to sit out for at least hour to hour and a half.

4. Place your loaf into a baking pan and bake in your oven for the next hour to hour and a half or until completely baked through.

Classic Monkey Bread

If you are looking for the perfect bread and dessert recipe to make for your next family gathering, then this is the perfect bread recipe for you. Easy to make and absolutely mouthwatering, I know your guests will be begging for more.

Makes: 12 Servings

Total Prep Time: 3 Hours and 20 Minutes

Ingredients:

- 2 ½ tsp. of Yeast, Active and Dry Variety
- 3 Cups of Flour, All Purpose Variety
- 1 tsp. of Cinnamon, Ground
- 1 tsp. of Salt, For Taste
- ¼ Cup of Sugar, White
- 2 Tbsp. of Butter, Soft
- 1 Cup of Water, Warm
- 1 Cup of Butter, Soft
- 1 Cup of Brown Sugar, Light and Packed
- 1 Cup of Raisins, Your Favorite Kind

Directions:

1. Add in your first 7 ingredients into your bread maker according to the directions suggested by the manufacturer.

2. Once your dough is completely mixed together and sticky to the touch, place onto a generously floured surface and knead for the next 10 minutes.

3. Then use a medium sized saucepan and place over low heat. Once your pan is hot enough add in your next 3 ingredients and cook until your butter is fully melted and your mixture is smooth in consistency. Remove from heat.

4. Next cut your loaf into small chunks and dip into your butter and brown sugar mixture. Place your coated chunks into a generously greased baking sheet.

5. Then place your dough in a warm area and allow to rise for the next 15 to 20 minutes.

6. After this time place into your oven to bake at 375 degrees for the next 20 to 25 minutes or until golden brown in color.

7. Remove from oven and flip face down onto a large sized plate. Serve while your bread is still warm and enjoy.

Hawaiian Style Bread

Once you get a taste of this bread you are going to feel as if you are sitting right on the black sanded beaches of this beautiful island. It is sweet to taste and absolutely delicious. I know you won't be able to get enough of it.

Makes: 15 Servings

Total Prep Time: 3 Hours and 10 Minutes

Ingredients:

- ½ Cup of Banana, Fully Mashed
- ½ Cup of Pineapples, Crushed and with Juice
- 1 Egg, Large in Size and Beaten
- ¼ Cup of Milk, Whole
- ¼ Cup of Butter, Soft
- 1 tsp. of Coconut Extract, Pure
- ½ tsp. of Salt, For Taste
- 1/3 Cup of Sugar, White
- ½ Cup of Potato Flakes, Instant Variety
- 3 Cups of Flour, Bread Variety
- 1 ½ tsp. of Yeast, Active and Dry Variety

Directions:

1. The first thing that you will want to do is grease your bread machine with some cooking spray.

2. Then add all of your ingredients into your bread maker according to the directions suggested by the manufacturer.

3. Once your dough is completely mixed together and sticky to the touch, place onto a generously floured surface and cover with some plastic wrap. Allow to sit out for at least hour to hour and a half.

4. Place your loaf into a baking pan and bake in your oven for the next hour to hour and a half or until completely baked through.

Italian Style Breadsticks

If you are a fan of Olive Garden Breadsticks, then I know you are going to love this delicious breadstick recipe. With the help of your bread machine you will be able to make these breadsticks in record time and be able to enjoy them that much faster.

Makes: 18 Servings

Total Prep Time: 3 Hours and 30 Minutes

Ingredients:

- 1 1/3 Cups of Water, Warm
- 3 Tbsp. of Butter, Soft
- 4 Cups of Flour, Bread Variety
- 2 tsp. of Salt, For Taste
- ¼ Cup of Sugar, White
- ¼ Cup of Sesame Seeds
- 2 Tbsp. of Milk, Dry and Powdered Variety
- 2 ½ tsp. of Yeast, Active and Dry Variety

Directions:

1. Add all of your ingredients into your bread maker according to the directions suggested by the manufacturer.

2. Once your dough is completely mixed together and sticky to the touch, place onto two generously greased baking sheet with a generous amount of cooking spray.

3. Then preheat your oven to 375 degrees.

4. Next place your dough onto a lightly oiled surface and divided into 18 equal sized pieces.

5. Roll your dough pieces into equal sized breadsticks and place onto your greased baking sheets, making sure to place them at least 1 inch apart.

6. Place into your oven to bake for the next 10 to 15 minutes or until golden brown in color.

7. Remove from your oven and place onto a wire rack to cool slightly before serving.

Simple Sourdough

Who doesn't love the taste of sourdough? If you are a huge fan of sourdough bread, then this is the perfect bread recipe for you to make.

Makes: 12 Servings

Total Prep Time: 3 Hour and 5 Minutes

Ingredients:

- ¾ Cup of Water, Warm
- 1 Cup of Sourdough, Starter Variety
- 1 ½ tsp. of Salt, For Taste
- 2 2/3 Cup of Flour, Bread Variety
- 1 ½ tsp. of Yeast, Dry and Active Variety

Directions:

1. Then add all of your ingredients into your bread maker according to the directions suggested by the manufacturer.

2. Once your dough is completely mixed together and sticky to the touch, place onto a generously floured surface and cover with some plastic wrap. Allow to sit out for at least hour to hour and a half.

3. Place your loaf into a baking pan and bake in your oven for the next hour to hour and a half or until completely baked through.

4. Remove from oven and allow to cool slightly before slicing.

Easy Bubble Bread

This is a nice and easy bread recipe that is easily made using your bread machine. This is another classic twist on traditional Monkey Bread that you won't be able to help but enjoy.

Makes: 10 Servings

Total Prep Time: 1 Hour and 15 Minutes

Ingredients:

- 1 Egg, Large in Size and Beaten Thoroughly
- 2 Tbsp. of Butter, Soft
- ½ Cup of Water, Warm
- ½ Cup of Milk, Warm
- 1 tsp. of Salt, For Taste
- 1 Tbsp. of Sugar, White
- 2 ½ Cups of Flour, Bread Variety
- 1 Pack of Yeast, Active and Dry Variety
- ¼ Cup of Butter, Fully Melted
- 1 tsp. of Paprika
- ¼ Cup of Parmesan Cheese, Finely Grated
- ½ tsp. of Garlic, Powdered Variety
- 1 tsp. of Onion, Dried and Minced
- ½ tsp. of Tarragon, Dried Variety

Directions:

1. The first thing that you will want to do is add your first 8 ingredients into your bread machine and start a cycle according to the manufacturer's instructions.

2. Next place your melted butter into a small sized bowl.

3. Then use a separate small sized bowl and mix together your remaining ingredients.

4. Next cut your dough into 20 to 25 equal sized pieces and roll in your melted butter. Roll next into your cheese mixture and place into a greased Bundt pan.

5. Cover with a damp clean cloth and allow to rise for the next 30 minutes or until your dough has doubled in size.

6. While your dough is rising, preheat your oven to 350 degrees.

7. After your dough has risen bake in your oven for the next 30 to 35 minutes or until golden in color.

8. Remove from oven and allow to cool slightly before serving.

Classic Italian Bread

This is an easy bread machine recipe that you can make to go along with your next Italian inspired meal. It tastes exactly as if it were made in the heart of Italy.

Makes: 12 Servings

Total Prep Time: 2 Hours and 40 Minutes

Ingredients:

- 3 Cups of Flour, All Purpose Variety
- 1 Tbsp. of Brown Sugar, Light and Packed
- 1 ½ tsp. of Salt, For Taste
- 1 1/8 Cups of Water, Warm
- 1 ½ Tbsp. of Olive Oil, Extra Virgin Variety
- 1 ½ tsp. of Yeast, Active and Dry Variety
- 1 Egg, Large in Size and Beaten
- 1 Tbsp. of Water, Warm
- 1 Tbsp. of Sesame Seeds
- 1 Tbsp. of Cornmeal

Directions:

1. First place all of your ingredients except for your last 4 ingredients into your bread machine in the order directed by the manufacturer.

2. Once your dough is completely mixed together and sticky to the touch, divide it into 2 equal sized pieces and form into even sized loaves.

3. Then sprinkle your cornmeal onto a lightly greased baking sheet and place your loaves directly onto it.

4. Brush your loaves with some water and allow to rise for the next 50 minutes.

5. While your dough is rising preheat your oven to 375 degrees.

6. After this time brush your loaves with your egg and sprinkle generously with some sesame seeds.

7. Cut 4 deep diagonal cuts into your bread.

8. Place a pan of hot water into your oven and place under your bread.

9. Bake your bread for the next 25 to 30 minutes or until golden in color.

10. Remove and allow to cool before slicing. Enjoy.

Simple Challah Bread

Here is yet another challah bread recipe that will soon become a favorite in your household. It is absolutely delicious and surprisingly easy to make.

Makes: 15 Servings

Total Prep Time: 3 Hours and 5 Minutes

Ingredients:

- 7/8 Cup of Water, Warm
- ½ Tbsp. of Salt, For Taste
- ¼ Cup of Honey, Raw
- 2 Eggs, Large in Size and Beaten
- ¼ Cup of Butter, Fully Melted
- 4 Cups of Flour, All Purpose Variety
- 2 tsp. of Yeast, Active and Dry Variety

Directions:

1. Add all of your ingredients into your bread maker according to the directions suggested by the manufacturer.

2. Once your dough is completely mixed together and sticky to the touch, divide your dough into 4 equal sized pieces.

3. Braid your pieces together and tuck the ends underneath, making sure to pinch with your fingers to seal.

4. Place your dough onto a generously greased baking tray and allow to rise for the next 30 minutes or until the dough has doubled in size.

5. While your dough is rising preheat your oven to 350 degrees.

6. After this time place your loaf into a baking pan and bake in your oven for the next 35 to 45 minutes or until deep golden brown in color.

7. Remove from oven and allow to cool completely before serving.

Italian Style Cheese Bread

This is a classic and strong bread to make if you are a cheese enthusiast. It pairs excellently with a classic Italian inspired dish. It will help to bring the entire meal together.

Makes: 12 Servings

Total Prep Time: 2 Hours and 15 Minutes

Ingredients:

- 1 ¼ Cups of Water, Warm
- 3 Cups of Flour, Bread Variety
- ½ Cup of Pepper Jack Cheese, Finely Shredded
- 2 tsp. of Italian Seasoning, Fresh
- 1 tsp. of Black Pepper, For Taste
- 2 Tbsp. of Parmesan Cheese, Finely Grated
- 2 Tbsp. of Brown Sugar, Light and Packed
- 1 ½ tsp. of Salt, For Taste
- 2 tsp. of Yeast, Active and Dry Variety

Directions:

1. The first thing that you will want to do is grease your bread machine with some cooking spray.

2. Then add all of your ingredients into your bread maker according to the directions suggested by the manufacturer.

3. Once your dough is completely mixed together and sticky to the touch, place onto a generously floured surface and cover with some plastic wrap. Allow to sit out for at least hour to hour and a half.

4. Place your loaf into a baking pan and bake in your oven for the next hour to hour and a half or until completely baked through.

Classic Kolaches

Kolaches are a great tasting dessert dish that I know your entire family will enjoy. This is a great dish to get the entire family involved with making and it will satisfy their strongest sweet teeth.

Makes: 24 Servings

Total Prep Time: 2 Hours and 5 Minutes

Ingredients:

- 1 ¼ Cups of Water, Warm
- ½ Cup of Butter, Soft
- 1 Egg, Large in Size and Beaten
- 1 Egg, Yolk Only
- 1/3 Cup of Milk, Powdered Variety
- ¼ Cup of Potato Flakes, Mashed and Instant Variety
- ¼ Cup of Sugar, White
- 1 tsp. of Salt, For Taste
- 3 7/8 Cups of Flour, Bread Variety
- 2 tsp. of Yeast, Active and Dry Variety
- 1, 12 Ounce Can of Pie Filling, Cherry Variety
- 1, 12 Ounces Can of Filling, Poppy seed Variety
- ¼ Cup of Butter, Fully Melted

Directions:

1. Add all your first 10 ingredients into your bread maker according to the directions suggested by the manufacturer.

2. Once your dough is completely mixed together and sticky to the touch, divide your dough with a tablespoon and roll into walnut shaped balls and place onto a generously greased cookie sheet, making sure they are at least 1 inch apart.

3. Cover with some plastic wrap and allow to rise for the next hour or until the balls have doubled in size.

4. Then flatten your balls and make a small depression right into the center using your thumbs. Fill each ball with your fills and cover again. Allow to rise for another 30 minutes.

5. While your dough is rising preheat your oven to 375 degrees.

6. After this time place your balls into your oven to bake for the next 13 to 15 minutes or until light brown in color.

7. After this time remove from your oven and brush with your melted butter. Place onto a wire rack and allow to cool before serving.

Savory Sun Dried Tomato Focaccia

With this classic bread machine recipe, you aren't just getting a loaf of bread, you are getting a huge meal as well. This focaccia is great to make tasty panini recipes or to enjoy by itself. Either way I know you are going to love it.

Makes: 6 Servings

Total Prep Time: 2 Hours and 5 Minutes

Ingredients:

- 1 Cup of Water, Warm
- 3 Cups of Flour, Bread Variety
- 2 Tbsp. of Milk, Dry and Powdered Variety
- 3 ½ Tbsp. of Sugar, White
- 1 tsp. of Salt, For Taste
- 3 Tbsp. of Butter, Soft
- 2 tsp. of Yeast, Active and Dry Variety
- ½ Cup of Tomatoes, Sun Dried Variety and Finely Chopped
- 2 Tbsp. of Olive Oil, Extra Virgin Variety
- 2 Tbsp. of Parmesan Cheese, Finely Grated
- 2 tsp. of Rosemary, Dried and Finely Crushed
- 1 tsp. of Garlic, Salted Variety
- 1 Cup of Mozzarella Cheese, Finely Shredded

Directions:

1. Add your first 8 ingredients into your bread maker according to the directions suggested by the manufacturer.

2. Once your dough is completely mixed together and sticky to the touch, place onto a generously floured surface and knead for the next minutes. Then cover with a damp cloth and allow to rise for the next 15 minutes.

3. While your dough is rising, dust a large sized baking dish with some cornmeal and roll out your dough so that it fits in the pan.

4. Brush your dough with some oil and cover again with a damp cloth. Allow to rise for an additional 30 minutes.

5. After this time sprinkle your dough with your remaining ingredients.

6. Then place into your oven to bake at 400 degrees for the next 15 minutes or until brown in color.

7. Remove and cool slightly before serving. Enjoy.

Conclusion

Well, there you have it!

Hopefully by the end of this book I hope you have learned not only how to make over 25 of the most delicious and nutritious bread machine recipes that you ever come across, but I also hope that you have learned what it really takes to make a delicious bread loaf by using this nifty kitchen tool.

So, what is next for you?

The next step to begin taking is to begin making all of the bread recipes that you have found in this book. Once you have mastered the art of making bread in the bread machine, then the next thing you want to do is to begin experimenting with making your own bread recipes. Feel free to use whatever kind of ingredients that you wish to truly make your next bread loaf unique.

Good luck!

About the Author

Martha is a chef and a cookbook author. She has had a love of all things culinary since she was old enough to help in the kitchen, and hasn't wanted to leave the kitchen since. She was born and raised in Illinois, and grew up on a farm, where she acquired her love for fresh, delicious foods. She learned many of her culinary abilities from her mother; most importantly, the need to cook with fresh, homegrown ingredients if at all possible, and how to create an amazing recipe that everyone wants. This gave her the perfect way to share her skill with the world; writing cookbooks to spread the message that fresh, healthy food really can, and does, taste delicious. Now that she is a mother, it is more important than ever to make sure that healthy food is available to the next generation. She hopes to become a household name in cookbooks for her delicious recipes, and healthy outlook.

Martha is now living in California with her high school sweetheart, and now husband, John, as well as their infant daughter Isabel, and two dogs; Daisy and Sandy. She is a stay at home mom, who is very much looking forward to expanding their family in the next few years to give their daughter some siblings. She enjoys cooking with, and for, her family and friends, and is waiting impatiently for the day she can start cooking with her daughter.

For a complete list of my published books, please, visit my Author's Page...

https://www.amazon.com/author/martha-stephenson

Author's Afterthoughts

Thanks ever so much to each of my cherished readers for investing the time to read this book!

I know you could have picked from many other books but you chose this one. So a big thanks for downloading this book and reading all the way to the end.

If you enjoyed this book or received value from it, I'd like to ask you for a favor. Please take a few minutes to post an honest and heartfelt review on Amazon.com. Your support does make a difference and helps to benefit other people.

Thanks!

Martha Stephenson

Made in the USA
Middletown, DE
12 November 2016